GOAL SETTING TO IMPROVE YOUR POTENTIAL & SELF-IMAGE

BY KNOWING WHAT YOU WANT, YOU WILL BE ABLE TO ACHIEVE IT AND MORE, EMPOWERING YOURSELF!

Lesley Meyer

CONTENTS

DREAMS AND GOAL SETTING

I have been using goal setting for many years. It was something that I was taught on one of the courses I attended. It has been most helpful having a clear idea of what I have wanted to achieve for the year. Amazing things happened when I planned each day and each night gave thanks for what I had received.

Many people do not set goals because they do not know what that means. In this book, I will elaborate on what goal setting is and how to achieve your dreams of what you want to do, have or become. When you start succeeding in

your goals, it will boost your self-esteem, making you a better person.

Research has shown that by writing your goals and dreams down and regularly reading them you will achieve 80-90% of them. [1]This will enable you to earn ten times more than those who do not.

The most valuable asset you possess in this world is yourself. God has given us the gifts, talents and resources to make our dreams a reality. Fear is often what keeps us from achieving our dreams and goals. If you see FEAR as the acronym: False Evidence Appearing Real, then you can choose whether you take action to overcome your fears and achieve your goals or not.

You must be willing to put in the effort to make your dreams happen. [2] You can't sit back and expect to achieve your dreams or have it given to you on a golden platter. By constantly thinking positive thoughts you are able to inspire yourself to take the action to achieve your dreams. If you constantly believe you are not worthy, not good enough and allow others to steal your dreams, then you will never reach your true potential and will feel regret. Whichever you believe, positive or negative, will be your reality.

As a student, you have your whole life in front of you and if you can start setting yearly goals as to what you want to achieve, you will be leaps ahead of the pack. As you are still at school and your subjects are set up for you each year, your goals might be as simple as achieving a specific mark for each subject. By putting in the daily effort to do your homework, you will be able to achieve what you have set out to do. When it's time to choose your subjects in high

school, you need to know what you want to become so that you can choose the right subjects to get there. If you are uncertain, have an aptitude test done. There are websites that describe the different professions which could help you make a decision.

I had a patient who lost her father when she was a little girl. Her mother was a stay at home mom and had to suddenly go and find work to support the two of them. She wanted to become a teacher, but they did not have money to pay for school fees. She heard that bursaries were available. She had a dream and all she had to do was put the work in.

She worked really hard at school and read books every day. Each test was a success and each year she achieved top marks in her class and was rewarded with a scholarship for the following year. School went by and she did so well that she was accepted into university. She worked full time and studied part-time to put herself through college and is now a qualified teacher.

This goal did not happen over-night, as no goal happens over-night. It took many years of hard work. Some goals do not take as long but all take time, dedication and hard work. You must let your marks work for you and not land up working for your marks. What I mean by this is; if you have good marks then you can choose what you would like to do with your future, be it going to university, starting your own business or getting a good job. If you do not have good marks, then you don't get the opportunity to choose and you must take what is given to you.

Only you are responsible for your future. Your success is the harvest of your hard work and thinking. You will reap what you have sown.

If you put in the work and diligently by keeping up to date with your homework, then your marks should be good. You will understand the material better and exams or tests will be easy. If you do not do your work diligently then you might not do as well as you had hoped.

THE 5 P'S
PRIOR PREPARATION PREVENTS POOR PERFORMANCE

It is said that the average person spends more time planning their holidays than they do planning their lives. It should be the other way round.

One should know what you are doing each day, each week, each year. Time should be set aside to plan this to make your life less stressful and prevent poor performance. Preparation is easily done with the help of Google (for your projects) and the use of a diary for your day to day activities and important dates. If you know when each project, test or exam is due, you are able to plan ahead and work on these subjects during the times you have available. If not, you land up scrambling at the last minute to get something done which results in you not getting the mark you wanted and feeling more stressed.

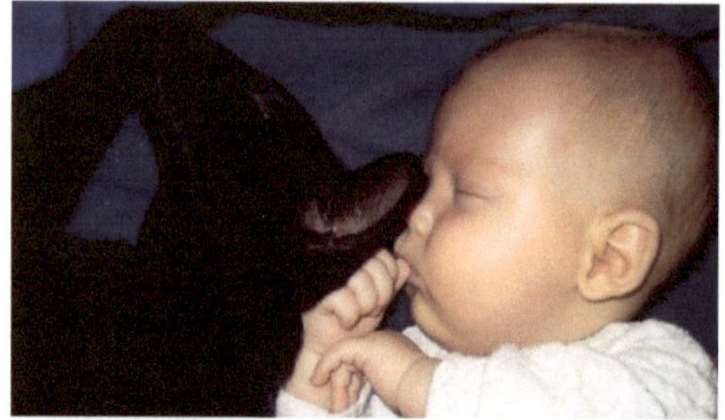

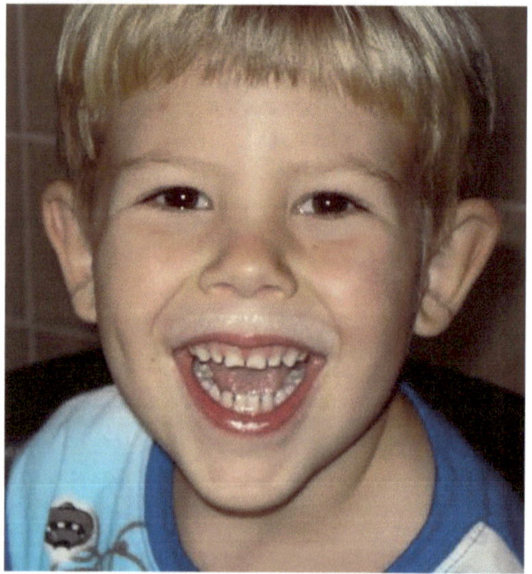

You need to be able to plan each day so that you have a combination of school, sport or after school activities and homework. Making a balance of work hard, rest hard and play hard! Spend a little time going the extra mile by doing perhaps another ten to twenty minutes of Math's to help you understand the subject better. Improving your reading will enhance your understanding of the questions asked in the exams. It will improve the speed at which you read, giving you more time to check your answers at the end of the test.

You may reward yourself by playing with your iPad, watching a nice movie or inviting a friend over to play. It is important to have this balance in your life. If you can get this balance right starting from when you are at school, you will set your life up for success in the future and avoid health complaints arising from stress.

Start how you mean to end: If you want to achieve good results you need to start at the beginning of the year and work hard throughout the year. Try something new each year to broaden your knowledge. You may find something that you are really passionate about. If you do not try something, then how do you know if you like it or not? Schools offer a range of different sports and cultural activities. Try playing a musical instrument, join the choir, play a sport or learn how to play chess. You need to do them for at least two years before you will be any good at them.

We are not born able to do sports, draw or play the piano. By trying these different activities we develop ourselves into amazingly all rounded people that are able to talk to a variety of people about a variety of topics.

A study was done where they asked a group of people to draw a portrait of themselves. Many of them drew basic outlines and were adamant that they could not draw. Over a few days, they were taught techniques of drawing a portrait. At the end of the tutorial they were asked to draw a portrait of themselves again and the results were astounding. This shows that all you need to be able to do something is to be shown how to do it. Do you have a fixed mindset or a growth mindset? [3,4]

You are able to do many things, as long as you are healthy and have the energy to do them. This means that you must make sure you get enough sleep, which is a minimum of eight hours, but preferably ten hours a night if you are of school going age. If you get a good nights' sleep, then you will be much more productive the next day. If you are not getting enough sleep, you will sleep in class or sleep in the car. This will alter your sleep pattern and make you less sleepy when it is bedtime. If you need an alarm clock to wake you in the morning, then you are not getting enough sleep. Sleep is a good way to prepare your body for the next day at school.

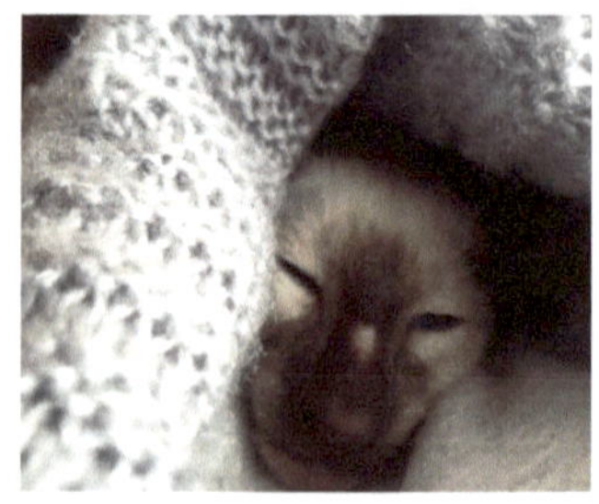

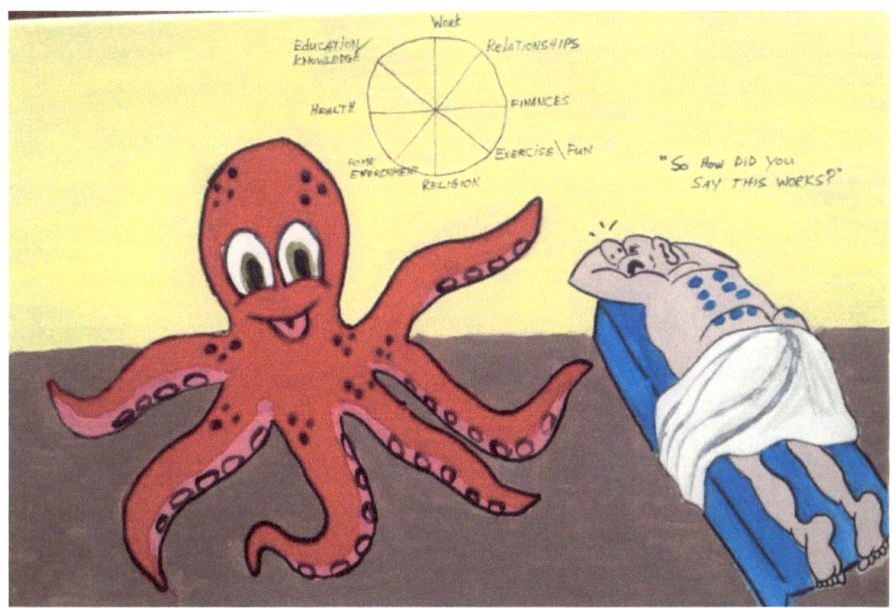

WHAT IS GOAL SETTING?

Goal setting is more than just a new year's resolution. It's a plan of action for the year. If you just go through your daily actions without knowing what you want out of life, then you will have to be happy with what life has dealt you. Goal setting is where you take time out, be it a day or a week, to analyze where you are in your life and what you want out of your life in the next year to five years. It's using the five Ps.

It is about what type of person you would like to become, what sports or extramural activities you would like to take part in. It's about what you would like to do in the future to make our world a better place. It's about thinking of a hundred things that you would like to do, be or have. Almost like a bucket list.

When you are little this sounds like a silly thing to do because surely what goals can you achieve? All you know is that your parents make you go to school, for who knows why and for such a long period of time. You would probably much rather stay home all day and play on the iPad.

School is very important as it teaches you how to read, write and think. It teaches you how to be a team player, to be polite and what is right and wrong. Having a good education opens the door to other opportunities, as you meet many people at school and network with those people. The only difference between a person who is able to read and one who is not is whether the person who can read uses this talent to better their circumstances and education as leaders are readers.

If you are struggling, do a little extra work in the subject you are struggling with. It works the same as the self-portrait information. When you put the effort in it becomes enjoyable. It is your responsibility to do the work, it is your future that you hold in your hands and the sooner you take ownership the better your life will be.

When you take part in goal setting, you can shape your life into one that is amazing. If you don't take part in goal setting you will be pushed in a direction that society pushes you into. Perhaps you land up in a group of children who take drugs or throw their lives away doing things that they should not be doing. By doing these negative activities you may make your life harder than it already is.

Your parents aren't responsible for your happiness, you are. Your parents may be poor but that doesn't mean you have to be. You may be living in an abusive environment, but that doesn't always have to be like that. You can choose what you want to happen. You have to sit down, think about where you are, what you want out of life and what you are going to do to get there.

Remember that your parents are doing the best that they can with the knowledge that they have at this moment in time. It's up to you to make the best out of what is available to you.

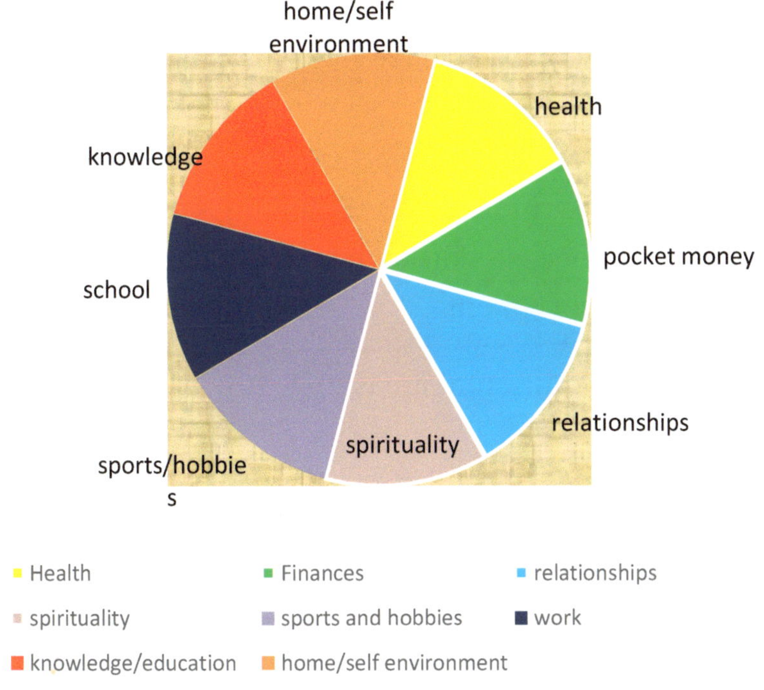

HOW GOAL SETTING IS DONE

Sometimes it is difficult to know where to begin when goal setting. What I have done here is take a pie chart and divide it up into the different sections of our lives. You take each section separately and rank it on a scale from 0-10 to determine how good or bad that area of your life is.

0 is dreadful and 10, is really great.

For each section, you will take the time to think about what you would like to be, do or have. See if you can write down five to ten goals or wishes for each section. The more you write the more you will think of and the more your brain will start looking for ways in achieving the goals. Once you have done this you will then take the two areas that have the lowest rating for you and focus on what you can do to improve their ratings by working towards achieving the goals you have written down. Sometimes the answers will automatically come, so don't worry too much about how you are going to achieve them.

Let's discuss the different areas in detail:

HEALTH

When your health is compromised you will find it hard to do any of the other areas as you cannot concentrate, exercise or work hard. This section is the most important area.

What does healthy mean? You need to feel energetic, awake all day and have a healthy body and mind. Your gut needs to go to the toilet every day and you must be able to sleep well each night, feeling rested the next day. You must be able to concentrate during class without your mind wandering, feeling tired or hyperactive. You need to feel happy and excited about going to school and not feel anxious, irritated or sad. You must be happy interacting with the children and teachers at school and not be nasty towards them.

To achieve good health, you need to eat healthy meals to keep your blood sugar levels constant, keep you awake and provide you with enough energy. You need to be able to take part in the sport without pains in your body and you need to ensure you drink enough good quality water. Your mind should be positive most of the time.

If you do not have a healthy body you will struggle to have a healthy mind and you will not achieve the goals you set out to do. Diet is the most important aspect that can change the way you look, feel and think. It can even improve your marks by 10% when you avoid foods that are unhealthy.

Which areas do you need to improve?

1: Sleep (8-12 hours depending on your age)
2: Diet (Avoid High GI and sugars)

3: Exercise (10 000 steps per day)

4: Gut movement (Daily)

5: Thoughts (Positive)

6: Water intake (your weight in KG x 0.03L water = amount of water you should be drinking per day)

High GI (Gluten index) means when a food such as bread, pasta, cakes and other starchy foods break down quickly into a sugar which causes inflammation in your body.

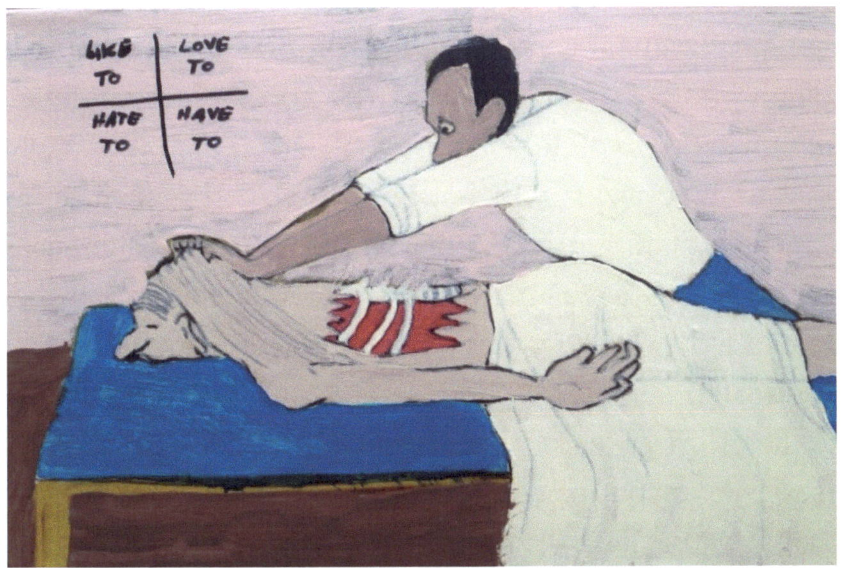

POCKET MONEY

I believe that one should earn your money even if it is only pocket money. If there is something special that you want to buy, then you must find a way to earn that money other than begging for it from your parents or stealing.

You need to learn how to work with money and the importance of only buying something that you can afford. In Robert Kiyosaki' s book *"Rich dad Poor dad"*, he says that you should take your monthly salary or in your case your pocket money and divide it as follows: 30% you use to restock your business, 30% you pay to yourself as a salary, 10% you put away for your pension, 10% you pay as tithes, 10% you use to improve your education and the last 10% you save towards buying or doing something that you really want to do.

To earn pocket money you need to look for something that is age appropriate and something that won't cost too much money to start. If you take a job, you start at the bottom and work your way up. It will not be a managerial position as you are not qualified to do the work. You may start as a packer or a waitress and as you get to understand the job, you could work your way up to the managerial position over a period of time. This is only if you put in the work and make the effort to learn what the next role entails and go on courses to give you the correct education.

Perhaps you can grow and sell plants and create your own nursery or plant and sell vegetables. Perhaps you could house sit, babysit or bake cakes and sell them. You can help cut the neighbours grass over Christmas or wash your neighbours' cars. If you are good at a subject, offer to coach others in your class for a small fee or help with skin care if you have good products to offer.

RELATIONSHIPS

There are many books out there that can help you in this area. Some of my favourites are *"Personality Plus" by Florence Littauer*. [5] This book talks about the different personalities and what their likes and dislikes are. If you know what type of person you are and your friends are, it is easier to deal with them. This book explains the Choleric /Melancholy /Sanguine /Phlegmatic-personalities. [5,6] There is a questionnaire that you can complete which will tell you your personality type. It points out your weaknesses, your strengths and how to work with others.

The other book that is useful is: *"The 5 love languages" by Gary Chapman*;[7,8] where he speaks about how different people feel loved and validated. At the beginning of each relationship, you tend to do all the different love languages as you want to impress the other person. When you are in your comfort zone you stop the other love languages and focus on your own love language.

The five love languages are gifts, quality time, positive affirmations, deeds, and touch. [7] If you are a gift person, you will like to give and receive gifts. If you are not a gift person, then the gifts won't really make you feel loved. If you are a touch person, you like to give and receive hugs. If you are not getting your quota of hugs, then you feel unloved.

The book talks about an empty love tank. [7,8] This empty love tank results in you finding this love in other places that are not necessarily good or the right thing to do. This is why it is so important to make sure you know what your love language is so that you know how to get it filled in the right way by the right people. The thing that you usually complain about is usually your love language that has not been fulfilled. So you feel unloved and have an empty love tank.

The same applies to your parents, so keep your ears open to what they are complaining about. If you start showing love to them, they will reciprocate the love and vice versa.

This is easy enough to resolve. By doing the test at the back of the *"The 5 love languages"* book or online you can find out which love language each person in the house is. When you feel loved you are able to improve your self-esteem and reach your full potential according to the Maslow hierarchy of needs. [9]

Another method to improve relationships is to make sure you listen to other people when they speak. Listen to such a degree that you are able to repeat what they have said with the exact meaning. If you do not understand, you need to ask questions to get clarity.

Most of us feel frustrated when we feel we have not been heard or our words get twisted into something totally different. When this method is used it gives clarity and there can be no misunderstanding. When we listen to this degree we will be able to show empathy, love, caring, and understanding which is how we should be communicating.

This makes a positive impact on all relationships. This should be implemented daily with your family. At the end of each day, it is important to get the family together to discuss what happened in each person's day. This keeps communication open, makes you feel loved and validated and keeps the support system activated.

No one is taught how to keep a relationship going, you follow from example. You will tend to do what your parents did and if you didn't have very good role models, then it makes it rather difficult to have a good relationship. There are so many tools available for you today that it is possible to find another role model or a different viewpoint to the one you were brought up with. You get counselors, books, and friends who have great relationships. You just need to make the effort to change.

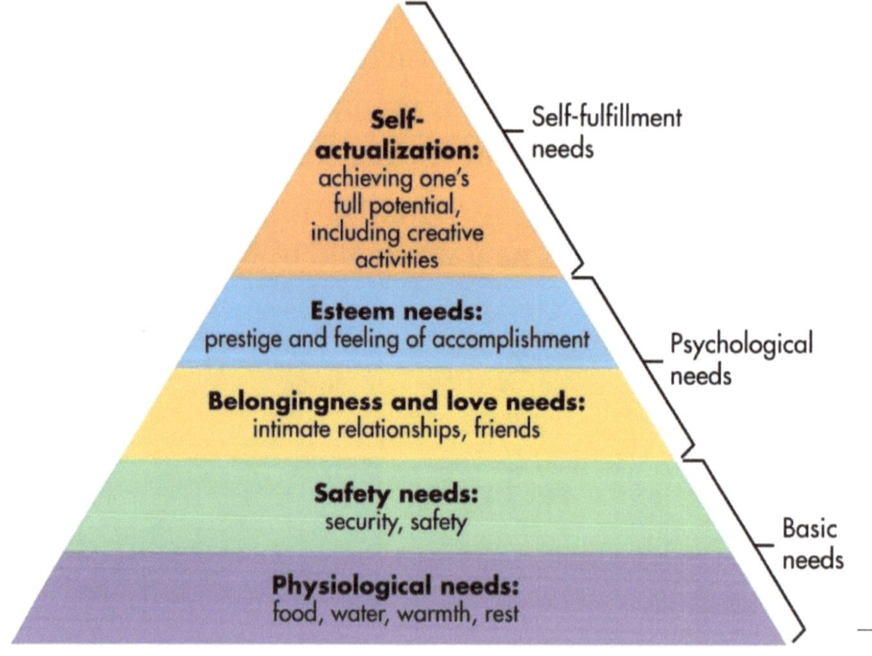

SPIRITUALITY

Here I don't necessarily mean going to church. If you spend quiet time being grateful for what you have, you will be given more to be grateful for. We underestimate the power of gratitude, the power of prayer and being quiet. When I started learning how to become quiet and meditate by clearing my mind, it was very difficult. I felt guilty for sitting around doing nothing. My aunt used to come and visit every Saturday. One Saturday we decided that we would begin to meditate. I have a few relaxing, guided meditation CDs which we used.

Five minutes into the music I had had enough and was fidgeting as I was uncomfortable but I sat still as my aunt was deep in meditation. It took me a year before I could drift away into quietness and sit for the entire CD.

Some people feel uncomfortable with the word meditation. Think of it as prayer or relaxation. Meditation is just getting your body and mind to be still, to think of nothing and just be in the moment. Meditation is the art of letting go, first in the body and then the mind. [10]

As our mind tends to wander, you can focus on a single thing. You could focus on your breathing or saying the words "OM". OM vibrates at a frequency of 432Hz which is the same vibration frequency as everything in nature. [11]

Meditation has been shown to improve your parasympathetic response in your body which is the healing response. Your sympathetic nervous system is the flight or fight system. Thus it is very important to activate your parasympathetic healing system. This is done through meditation, breathing, sleep, and massage, Chi Gung or Tai Chi, being outside in nature, being quiet and eating healthily. The important thing is to become quiet and clear your mind or only take in what is beautiful around you, creating infinite possibilities of positive things happening in your life.

SPORT AND HOBBIES

To be an all-rounder and ensure that your body is healthy, it is important to partake in sports and hobbies. At school, these are readily available to you and are a lot of fun when you get good at doing them. If you are not fit or you do not like doing sport, it is mostly because you are not good at it YET.

Sometimes one avoids doing sport because you are not healthy, are not good at it and you worry about what others will say. Perhaps you are overweight and it makes you too hot or triggers your asthma. Sport is very good for your body, in these situations; you would start slowly and stop to take a breather when you are tired. As you get fitter you will be pleased that you kept at it, as it will help you lose weight, improve your health as well as improve your self-confidence

and self-image. It will even improve your concentration and help you to sleep better.

Your aim is to do ten thousand steps per day. If you are unable to do ten thousand steps because of being unfit or unhealthy, start with what you can do and each week increase the number of steps taken until you reach the target.

There are some basic exercises you can add which strengthens your back, stomach, legs, and arms. They are push-ups, Pilates' sit-ups, bridging and squats. Ten of each every day and within six months you will see the difference in your body.

If you do not do any exercises you will pay the price later in life as your body will not be as strong and as fit as it should be. This can compromise your health. Exercises help improve bone growth and prevent Osteoporosis. Our bone is only laid down in areas that have rotational stress applied to the area from the exertion of the muscles pulling on the bone. [12] This only occurs when we do exercises that require the muscles to actively work. If you do not exercise, your bones become brittle and you may fracture (break) them without even falling. When they are this brittle you are said to have osteoporosis. [12]

Exercise will help you to play your musical instrument better as your muscles will have more strength and endurance to perform better. If you sit in front of the computer a lot, exercises will help prevent you from getting a poor posture and headaches. Exercise forms the base of the new food pyramid. [12]

THE HEALTHY EATING PYRAMID

Department of Nutrition, Harvard School of Public Health

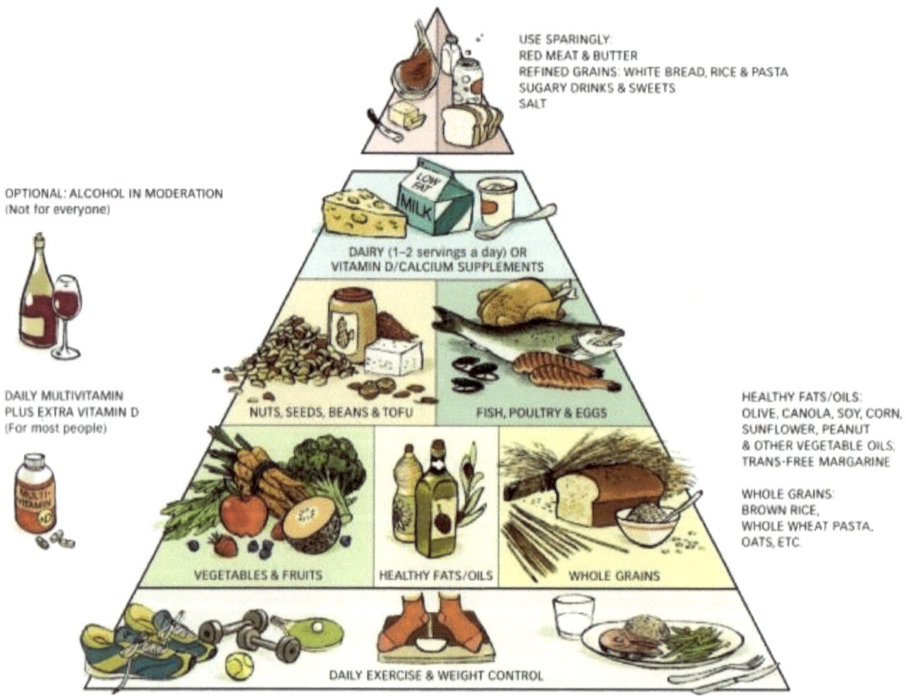

KNOWLEDGE AND EDUCATION

The brain is a muscle that must constantly be exercised and flexed to keep it strong and healthy. [13] By constantly trying out new challenges, reading books or doing Math, you are able to do this. Each year since I read *"Rich dad Poor dad,"* I have made a point of doing something new. I have done art, opera, modeling, photography, dog school, garden designing, Belly dancing and Stock market trading.

Using this knowledge and my previous knowledge, I have made all my own curtains, furniture covers, Belly dance outfits and medieval outfits. I have designed seven gardens and helped lay them out and provided the plants for them from Vincent's indigenous nursery. We set this nursery up for him to earn pocket money from. I have written a chronic pain book and am writing this series of books. I have a well-trained dog that is now a therapy dog and a garden that is designed to meditate and be quiet in. There is always something new to do using the knowledge that I have gained, making life fun and boosting my self-confidence and self-image.

At school, everything is offered to you. All you need to do is arrive for the activity. It is good to get into the habit of thinking about what other activities you would like to do in the future. By doing this you achieve many things and have a large background of information to draw information from. It makes you far more positive, interesting, educated and entertaining and people will want to be around you.

If you think about it, your entire school career is set up to teach you specific knowledge. When you go to university you are taught more in a specific field until you complete your degree. When you qualify or finish school, what do you do to improve yourself? In the medical field and some other fields, it has become law for us to continue our education in our field. However, there are many people out there that do nothing to further their knowledge, which means you stagnate where you are.

Leaders are readers and what gets measured improves. None of the knowledge you gain is wasted. Knowledge is power. Reading books will add to your self-growth as you will be the same person in the next five years that you are today, except for the people you hang around with, the books you read and the things you listen to. What does this mean? If you want to be successful then you need to hang around successful people. If you want to be knowledgeable then read books that will broaden your general knowledge. If you want to improve yourself in a specific field then find books, a tutor or listen to educational CDs. There are several free online courses that can provide you with the necessary education.

If you read books on a specific topic, within two years of reading twenty minutes per day, you will have gained the knowledge equivalent of a semester doing a PhD. *"Investment into knowledge is the only investment that yields the greatest return" Benjamin Franklin.*

SEUN VAN DIE WEEK
BOY OF THE WEEK
ST PAUL

SCHOOL

Many of my patients work too hard, feeling the stress of deadlines. They feel obliged to work all hours of the day just to get the work done. I have also noticed that school children are feeling more and more stressed as they feel that there is too much work for them to do.

If you are staying up late to finish your work because you have not planned properly, then you are going to get stomach ulcers, headaches or other medical problems. It boils down to getting the balance right. There is always enough time. Sometimes you need to play less on your iPad, watch less TV and work more. You don't need to take part in every single activity that the school has arranged. You need at least one sport per term and a hobby or two sports. More than this means you have less time to fit everything in.

I often say: "start how you mean to end!'" If you want to do well, then you need to start at the beginning of the year working hard. It also means that if you start a job and want to have time for your family, friends or exercise, then you should only work your working hours making time to fit the other activities in. The work never ends so don't try and do it all in one day, neglecting your health, family, and friends. Learn to say No and learn your limits.

Sitting down and focusing on your tasks at hand means you will be more productive and be able to complete what needs to be done in a timeous fashion. Procrastination is a killer in terms of productivity. By just starting you are able to complete a lot more than you thought you would be able to do. Time is very valuable. By working diligently during school you can get a lot of work done making more time for afternoon sports and free time over the weekends. *"Formal education will earn you a living and self-education will earn you a fortune"*. Jim Rohn

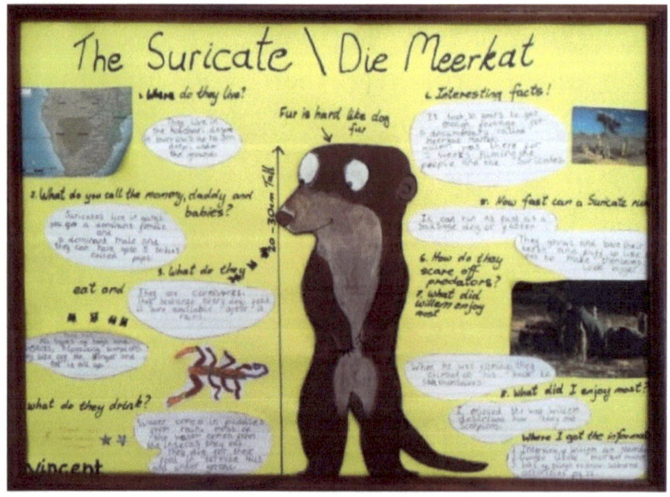

HOME AND SELF-ENVIRONMENT

This is something I added after a while of doing goal setting. I noticed that very few people actually have nice gardens or dress well. I felt it was something one needs to do.

Having a beautiful garden is rewarding in many ways: It provides you with a variety of activities to do, can give feelings of peace and contentment, beautiful flowers to admire and a menagerie of animals to watch as they bustle about their daily business. You are also more likely to invite people over as you do not feel embarrassed about your home.

Designing your garden is not too difficult and is easier to do on paper once you have your measurements. You can do it in small sections and watch it transform each season.

When you have a pretty home and garden, you want to be home. Your animals want to be home. This is what I mean by the home environment. This includes your house too. Is it sunny and welcoming or is it cluttered with rubbish? De-clutter, open it up and clean it out. If you do not know how to make your home beautiful, then find someone who does or likes to. You may even have a family member or friend that can come and help.

Clean your home every year. Go through the cupboards and get rid of all the old broken things or things you no longer wear and fix what you want to keep.

Everyone in the house must feel that the home is homely. You must want to go home, not avoid going home. A dirty home is very bad for your health physically and mentally.

Self-environment is how you dress, wear your hair and do your makeup. It has been said that it takes seven seconds to make a first impression. This is before you have even opened your mouth and greeted the person. So what kind of an impression do you want to leave?

Some people have a natural talent for dressing well and look good at any occasion. Maybe they could help you get a new wardrobe. There are people who study fashion design and

colour and style analysis. These people are able to look at your body shape, hair colour and skin colour, to determine you what you should and should not be wearing. If you are wearing the wrong colour but the right style, you can look sick and tired. Wearing the right colour and right style makes you look vibrant and alive.

It does not have to cost a lot but getting the right look will get you more compliments which will boost your self-confidence. You will spend less money on buying the wrong clothes.

ACHIEVING YOUR GOALS AND DREAMS

Having a dream or goal gives you a purpose, makes you feel that your life matters and that you are making a difference. If you want to achieve something you need to make a concrete plan for what you want to achieve. One doesn't always need to know how you are going to get it. But when you have a goal, your mind will be open to finding solutions and these will be brought to your attention, helping you find the how.

It takes one step at a time to get to where you want to be. It is your choice whether you will do it or not and your choice whether you are going to make your dreams a reality or not. Your life is in your hands. ***"We are what we repeatedly do. Excellence then is not an act, but a habit."*** Aristotle

If excellence is a habit, what habit would you like to start? It will take three weeks to make this action a habit. A year flies by so quickly. It would be better to look back and be pleased with the results you have achieved as opposed to wishing you were better, stronger, smarter, prettier, thinner etc.

Beauty comes from within when you know where you are going. When you do it with passion the positivity will automatically radiate from you. By taking on new challenges and succeeding at them, you will accept how you look and accept who you are. People will want to be around you and this will make you feel good about yourself. You will resonate with determination and enthusiasm which will produce the positive outcomes and success you desire.

"Everybody is a genius. But if you judge a fish by its ability to climb a tree it will live its whole life believing that it is stupid"-Albert Einstein.

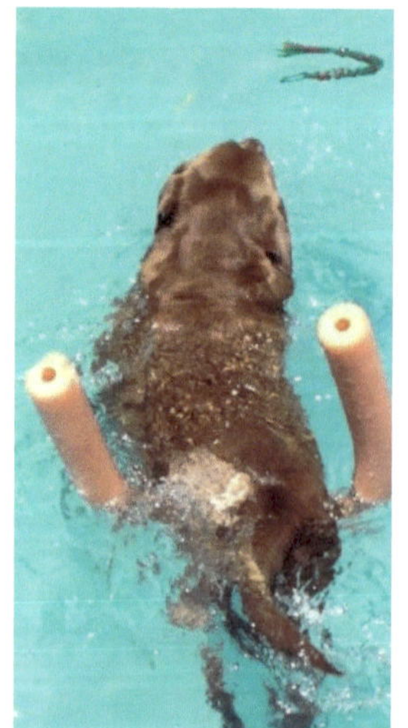

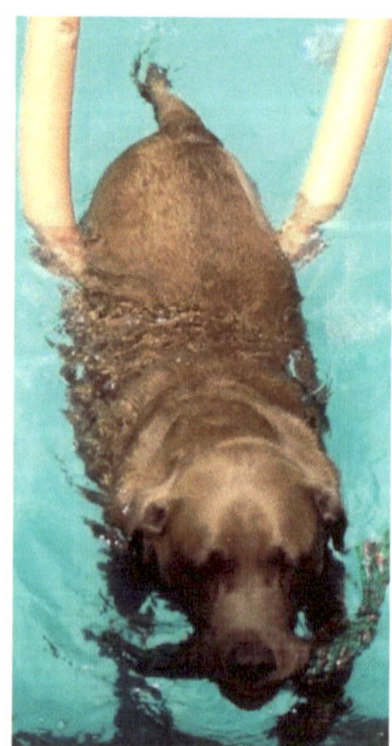

HELP ME COPE ACTIVITIES

1. What does goal setting mean to you?
2. Take your time to go through each area of the pie chart of goals and write five to ten goals for each area.
3. How are you going to prepare your daily schedule to work towards achieving these goals you have set?
4. Which are the two main areas that need the most attention in your life?
5. How are you going to go about improving these two areas?
6. What is the most important thing that you can do that could improve your health drastically?
7. What could you do, with the knowledge and ability that you already have, to earn pocket money?
8. Which love language fills your love tank?
9. What sport or hobby do you partake in or which would you like to try?
10. Which subject do you need help with; who can you ask to help you?
11. Do your home and garden look the way you would like it to look? How are you going to change this?
12. How can you improve your outward appearance?

REFERENCES

1. The Dominican University of California. Written goals study. Httpswwwdominicaneduacademicslaeundergraduate-Programspsychfacultyassets-Gail-Matthewsresearchsummary2pdf.

2. Del Sesto D. Shift Your Thinking: 200 Ways to Improve Your Life. [Internet]. Grand Rapids: Revell; 2016 [cited 2018 Aug 11]. Available from: http://public.eblib.com/choice/publicfullrecord.aspx?p=4448455

3. Dweck CS. Mindset: the new psychology of success. Ballantine Books trade pbk. ed. New York: Ballantine Books; 2008. 277 p.

4. How I learned to draw realistic portraits in only 30 days.

5. Littauer F. Personality plus. Rev. and expanded ed. Tarrytown, N.Y: F.H. Revell Co; 1992. 183 p.

6. Littauer F, Sweet R. Personality plus at work: how to work successfully with anyone. Grand Rapids, Mich: Revell; 2011. 267 p.

7. Chapman GD, Campbell R. The five love languages of children. Chicago: Moody Press; 1997. 224 p.

8. Chapman GD. The five love languages. Chicago: Northfield Pub; 1992. 175 p.

9. Tim van de Vall. Maslow's Hierarchy of needs. 2013.

10.   Swami Rama. What is the meaning of meditation? [Internet]. Available from: https://yogainternational.com/article/view/the-real-meaning-of-meditation

11.   Sam Saunders. OM: What is it and why do we chant it? [Internet]. 2013. Available from: https://www.mindbodygreen.com/0-7565/om-what-is-it-why-do-we-chant-it.html

12.   McCormick RK. The whole-body approach to osteoporosis: how to improve bone strength and reduce your fracture risk. Oakland, CA: New Harbinger Publications; 2008. 220 p.

13.   The Institute for Functional Medicine. Protecting the brain with exercise.

ABOUT THE AUTHOR

Lesley is a Physiotherapist with a special interest in chronic pain. She has studied extensively in a variety of different therapies to enable her to treat her patients holistically. Her studies have taught her the importance of goal setting which she does every year to set her mind straight and achieve everything that she wants to do and more. She uses the goal setting pie with all her patients with outstanding results and has taken the time to share it with anyone who is interested in reading this book to help inspire them to be and do more.

From the same author:

Tired of being tired to the point of being gatvol

Knights of the 21st century

Goal setting to improve your potential and self-image

How not to stress-out

Animals can be bullies too. Meet the anti-bully sheriff in town

The old "Finishing School"

Bphyst/APPI/EFT/DDN/IMS/OMT/NLC

1004 Rabie Road,

Eldoraigne X1,

Centurion

0157

South Africa

+(27)(0)825510388

Cope.sa@vodamail.co.za